SIMPLE MACHINE PROJECTS

Making Machines with Levers

Chris Oxlade

raintree

a Capstone company — publishers for children

Raintree is an imprint of Capstone Global Library Limited, a company incorporated in England and Wales having its registered office at 7 Pilgrim Street, London, EC4V 6LB – Registered company number: 6695582

www.raintree.co.uk
myorders@raintree.co.uk

Edited by James Benefield and Erika Shores
Designed by Steve Mead
Original illustrations © Capstone Global Library Ltd 2015
Picture research by Jo Miller
Production by Victoria Fitzgerald
Originated by Capstone Global Library Ltd
Printed and bound in China

ISBN 978 1 406 28926 8
18 17 16 15 14
10 9 8 7 6 5 4 3 2 1

British Library Cataloguing in Publication Data
A full catalogue record for this book is available from the British Library.

Acknowledgements
We would like to thank the following for permission to reproduce photographs:

All photos Capstone Studio: Karon Dubke except: Alamy: Caro, 18; Dreamstime: Puma330, 4, Vitaly Titov & Maria Sidelnikova, 29 (bottom); Photoshot/Eye Ubiquitous, 12; Shutterstock: Alenavlad, 25, c12, 27, John Kropewnicki, 19, roger pilkington, 29 (top), Vadim Ratnikov, 26; SSPL via Getty Images, 13; Wikimedia: Sébastien Savard, 24

Design Elements: Shutterstock: Timo Kohlbacher

We would like to thank Harold Pratt and Richard Taylor for their invaluable help in the preparation of this book.

Every effort has been made to contact copyright holders of material reproduced in this book. Any omissions will be rectified in subsequent printings if notice is given to the publisher.

All the internet addresses (URLs) given in this book were valid at the time of going to press. However, due to the dynamic nature of the internet, some addresses may have changed, or sites may have changed or ceased to exist since publication. While the author and publisher regret any inconvenience this may cause readers, no responsibility for any such changes can be accepted by either the author or the publisher.

CONTENTS

Some words are shown in bold, **like this**. You can find out what they mean by looking in the glossary.

WHAT IS A LEVER?

Have you cut paper with scissors or broken open a nut with nutcrackers? Then levers have helped you!

A lever is a simple machine. Simple machines make our lives easier by helping us to do jobs, such as lifting heavy loads, gripping objects and cutting materials. In this book, you'll see many examples of levers, and the activities will help you to understand how levers work.

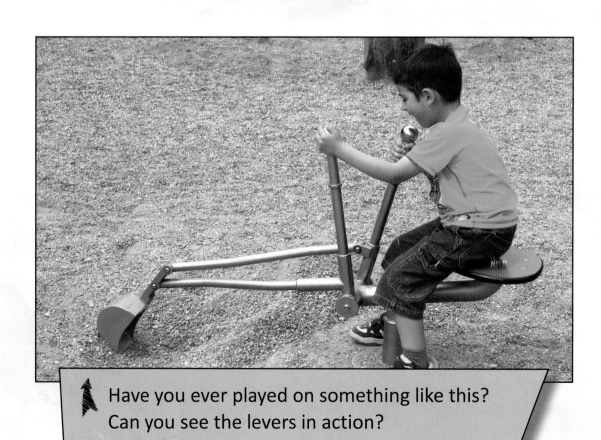

Have you ever played on something like this?
Can you see the levers in action?

Levers everywhere

Scissors and nutcrackers are just some of the household tools and gadgets that rely on levers to work. Other levers you might find in your house include tin openers, bottle openers, tap handles, hammers and pliers.

SIMPLE MACHINES

The other simple machines are the **pulley**, the **wheel and axle**, the **ramp** (and the **wedge**) and the **screw**. Also, **springs** are like simple machines.

fulcrum

bar of stiff material

 A lever is made up of a bar, fixed at a fulcrum (pivot).

HOW LEVERS WORK

When you push (or pull) on one part of a lever, the lever pushes (or pulls) on the object or material you want to move, squeeze or cut. A see-saw is a lever. One child's weight (how heavy they are) lifts another child's weight.

One lever or two?

Some tools, such as a bottle opener and a crowbar, are made up of a single lever. But many tools and gadgets, such as scissors and pliers, are made up of two levers joined together.

FORCE AND MOTION

Simple machines such as levers can change force and **motion**. A simple machine can make a force (a push or a pull) larger or smaller, or change the direction of a force. It can also make a movement larger or smaller, or change the direction of a movement.

Three types of levers

There are three different types of lever. In each type, the fulcrum, the place where you pull or push, and the position of the object being moved or cut, is different. The project on the next page will help you to understand what each type of lever does.

Pliers are first-class levers

Fulcrum

Nutcrackers are second-class levers

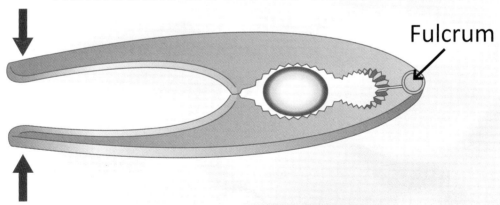

Fulcrum

Tweezers are third-class levers

Fulcrum

Three different levers

Here's how to make tools that use the three different types of lever (see page 7). You can test how each type of lever changes forces and motion.

A first-class lever

1 Place the pen on a table and rest the centre of the ruler on the pen. Use an elastic band to join the ruler and pen together, as shown.

STEP 1

2 Put one finger from each hand on each end of the ruler. Can you feel that when you push down with one finger, you push up the other finger?

STEP 2

Bigger forces

3 Now slide the pen along until it is about 5 cm from one end of the ruler. Put your fingers on the ends of the ruler again. Can you feel that a small downwards push on the long end makes a larger upwards push at the short end?

STEP 3

A second-class lever

4 Take the pen off the ruler. Get the second ruler and put the two rulers face to face, with the pen in between them, about 2 cm from one end.

5 Put an elastic band around the long ends of the rulers. Slide the elastic band along until it is next to the pen. Twist the elastic band and loop it over the short ends of the rulers.

STEP 5

6 Put a finger in between the rulers, close to the pencil. Squeeze the two ends together with the other hand. Do the levers change how much you push?

STEP 6

A third-class lever

7 Now put a finger between the ends of the rulers, and hold the rulers close to the pen with the other hand. What do the levers do to your push this time?

STEP 7

What did you find out?

This project shows that levers can be arranged in different ways to make forces bigger and smaller. First-class levers can make forces bigger or smaller, second-class levers always make forces bigger and third-class levers always make forces smaller.

LEVERS IN HISTORY

The lever is not a new idea! People understood levers thousands of years ago. They put them to work to do the same jobs they do today – to lift and move heavy things, and to squeeze and cut materials.

Lifting water

A shaduf is an ancient machine used to raise water. The weight of a big rock, and a pull from a farmer, on one end of a wooden lever lifts a heavy bucket of water on the other end of the lever. In some places, farmers still use this simple tool today.

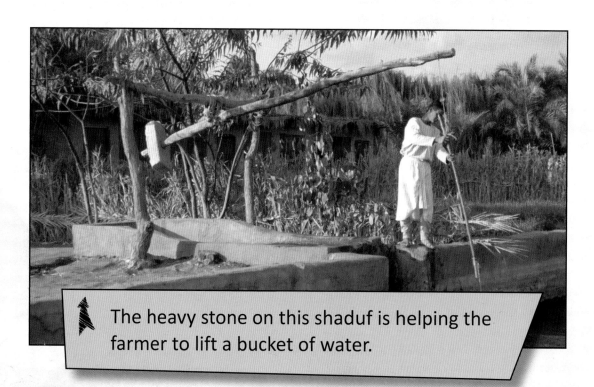

The heavy stone on this shaduf is helping the farmer to lift a bucket of water.

Weighing goods

Roman tradesmen weighed their goods with levers. A Roman **weighing machine** was made up of a metal bar suspended near the centre. A small weight was moved along the bar to make the bar balance.

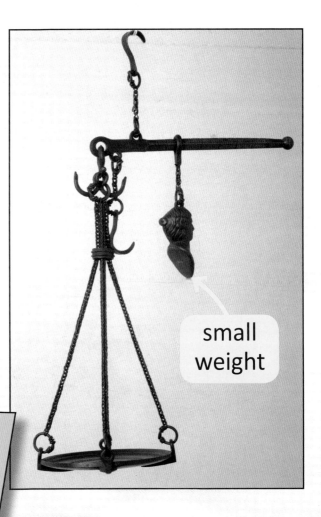

small weight

The position of the weight showed the size of the weight in the pan.

MOVING THE EARTH

The mathematician Archimedes, from ancient Greece, realized how powerful levers could be. He said that if he had a lever long enough and he had a place to put the fulcrum, he could move Earth with his hands.

Make some weighing scales

This project will show how a Roman weighing machine worked.

1 Cut out a thin rectangle from one side of the A4 card, as shown in the picture. You could use a ruler for accuracy.

STEP 1

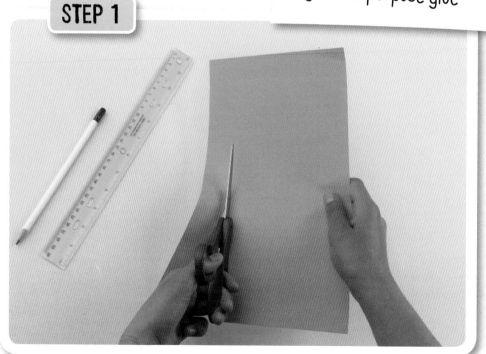

2 Put the card rectangle on top of the ruler. Tape it in place at the ends and at the middle.

STEP 2

3 Place the pencil on top of the ruler, in the centre of the ruler (see picture for step five).

4 Wrap an elastic band around the ruler and the pencil. This will keep the pencil and the ruler together (again, see the picture for step five).

5 Glue the plastic lid, upside down, onto the card, 5 cm from the pencil.

STEP 5

6 Rest the pencil on the two wooden blocks, as shown in the picture for step 7. Move the pencil along the ruler until the ruler balances.

7 Put one washer in the lid. Put another washer on the other end of the ruler. Move this washer backwards and forwards until the ruler balances.

STEP 7

8 Draw a line level with the centre of the washer, and write "1" next to the line.

9 Add another washer to the lid. Move the single washer to balance the ruler again. Make another mark, and write "2" next to it.

10 Repeat step 9, using three and then four washers in the lid. Now you have a scale on the ruler.

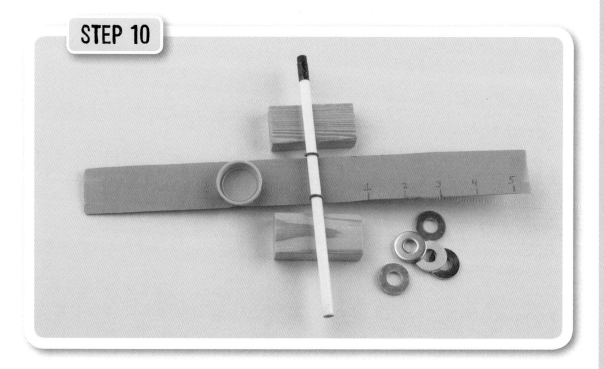

STEP 10

11 Put a small object in the lid. Move the single washer to balance the ruler. How many washers does your object weigh?

What did you find out?

The ruler works like a weighing machine. It shows how many washers an object weighs. The further along the ruler you have to move the single washer, the heavier the object in the tray is.

CHANGING FORCES AND MOTION

When you push or pull on one part of a lever, the lever makes a larger or smaller push on another object. But the further away from the fulcrum you push or pull, the bigger effect your push or pull has.

A wheel brace is a tool for tightening the wheel nuts on a car wheel. It has a very long handle, so a good push at the end of the brace does up the nut extremely tightly.

This wheel brace has two long levers so the driver can do up the wheel nuts very tightly.

An oar is a long lever. The fulcrum is the oar holder on the side of the boat.

Levers can also change motion, making a movement much greater. If you move one part of a lever a small distance, another part moves a much greater distance. Rowing is a good example. A rower pulls the handle of an oar a short distance and the blade of the oar (in the picture above, the orange end of the oar) moves much further through the water.

GIANT SPANNERS

The parts of a building's **steel frame** are joined together with huge nuts and bolts. Workers do up the nuts and bolts extremely tightly with very long **spanners**.

Magnifying motion

This project shows how levers can change motion, making a small movement into a large movement.

What you need:
- a piece of stiff card 30 cm x 20 cm (A4 size)
- some more stiff card
- a ruler
- a pen
- paper fasteners
- a sharp pencil

1 Cut two strips of card 20 cm x 3 cm, and one strip 15 x 3 cm.

2 In one of the 20 x 3 strips, pierce a small hole 5 cm from one end. Don't push the pencil right through. On the card, write "A" next to the hole. Then pierce a small hole 1.5 cm from the other end of the strip. Write "B" next to it. See picture below.

STEP 2

3 In the second 20 cm x 3 cm strip, pierce a hole 1.5 cm from one end. Write "E" next to it. Then make a second hole, hole "F", 5 cm along from Hole E.

4 In the last strip pierce a hole 1.5 cm from each end. Label the holes "C" and "D" (see the step 2 picture).

STEPS 4 AND 5

5 Connect holes B to C and holes D to E, with the paper fasteners.

STEPS 4 AND 5

6 Get the A4 card. Pierce a small hole 4 cm from one long edge (see picture). Pierce a hole 4 cm in from one corner on the other edge.

STEP 6

7 Connect the strips to the card with paper fasteners, through these holes. Experiment with paper fasteners to see where you need to place them.

STEP 7

8 Put your hand on a sheet of card and draw around it. Cut out the hand and tape it to the long card arm (see picture, right).

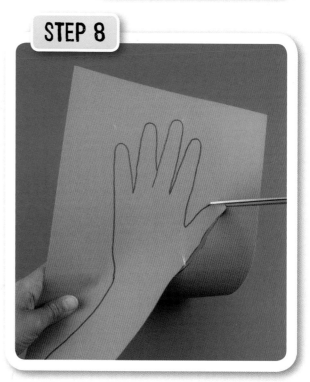

STEP 8

9 Move the lever arm (as shown, below) from side to side to make the hand wave!

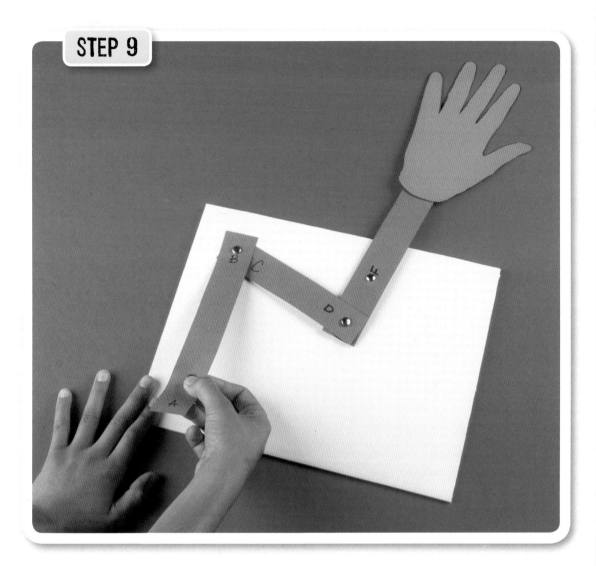

STEP 9

What did you find out?
Working together, the two levers make a small movement of your fingers into a much larger movement of the waving hand.

EVERYDAY LEVERS

We use levers in all sorts of places. Some, such as scissors, are easy to see, but others are not so obvious.

Cantilever bridges

Many bridges rely on levers to stay up. One sort of bridge that relies on the lever is the cantilever bridge. The bridge itself is a lever. One end of the lever stretches out over the water, and the other end is connected to the ground.

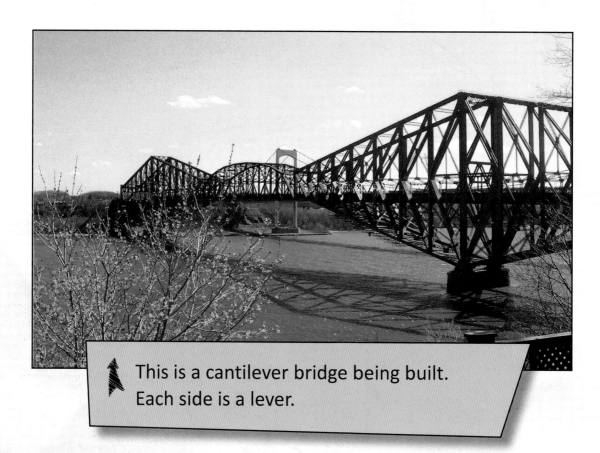

This is a cantilever bridge being built. Each side is a lever.

Some musical instruments rely on levers, too. All the keys on a piano keyboard are levers. So are the foot pedals. When you press a key down, the other end of the key pushes up. It presses on another lever called the hammer, and the hammer hits a string to play a note.

When a piano player presses on a key, levers make a hammer swing and hit a string to play a note.

LEVERS IN YOUR BODY

You even have levers in your body. Your lower arm is a lever. Your elbow is its fulcrum, and it is moved up and down by your bicep muscle in your upper arm.

LEVERS IN COMPLEX MACHINES

Many complicated machines contain simple machines such as levers. Construction machines such as diggers and cranes use levers to lift and move materials. The arm of a digger is made up of levers. In the driver's cab, there are levers that the driver uses to control the digger, to move the arm and digging bucket.

Hydraulic rams push and pull on one end of the levers in this digger's arm.

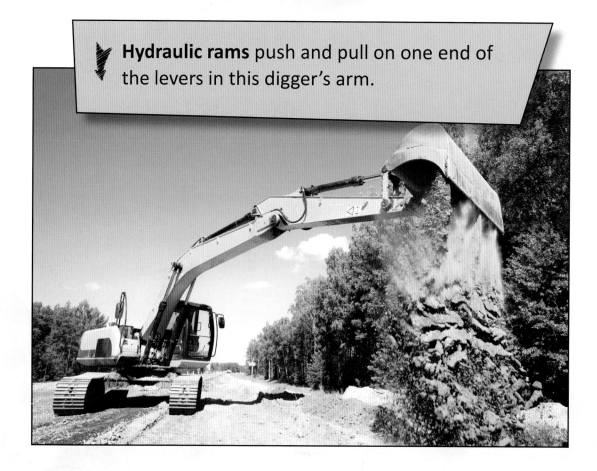

Bicycles also have levers. You pull brake levers on the handlebars, which pull cables attached to the brakes. At the brakes, the cables move levers that press rubber brake blocks onto the wheels to slow them.

Have a look on your own bicycle to see the levers that work the brakes.

THE LONGEST LEVERS

Booms are long arms of cranes. They act as super-long levers. A huge concrete weight on one end of the boom holds up the other end of the boom and the load hanging from it.

FACTS AND FUN

AMAZING LEVERS

The longest cantilever bridge in the world is the Pont de Quebec, in Quebec, Canada. It is 549 metres (1,801 feet) long.

There are even levers in space! The robot arm on the International Space Station is made up of thin levers, and is 17 metres (56 feet) long.

Humans are not the only creatures to use levers. Orang-utans use sticks as levers to open tasty fruits.

The longest see-saw in the world was built by Ashrita Furman of New York, USA. It is 24 metres (79 feet) long.

The Kroll K-10000 tower crane has an arm 100 metres (330 feet) long – it's the longest arm of any tower crane.

LEVERS TODAY

All simple machines, including levers, were invented thousands of years ago. The lever may have been invented around 200,000 years ago. It's amazing that levers are just as important today as they were then. We often use levers in complex modern machines, but also for the same jobs that people used them for all that time ago. And the lever will probably be useful for many years to come!

Where and what are these levers?

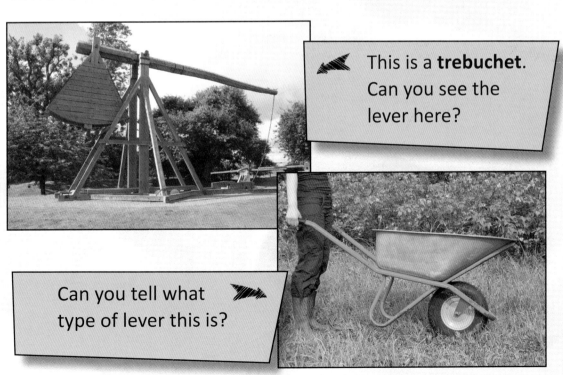

This is a **trebuchet**. Can you see the lever here?

Can you tell what type of lever this is?

GLOSSARY

fulcrum point around which a lever rotates

hydraulic ram piston pushed out of a cylinder by liquid, used to move parts of large machines such as diggers

motion another way of saying movement

pulley simple machine made up of wheels and rope, used to lift or pull objects

ramp simple machine used to lift heavy objects

screw simple machine that has a spiral-shaped thread, used to fix or lift materials

spanner tool for tightening or loosening a nut or bolt

spring device that can be pressed or pulled but returns to its first shape when released

steel frame steel skeleton that holds up a building

trebuchet medieval weapon. It works like a catapult.

wedge simple machine used to split apart materials

weighing machine machine that measures the force that pulls an object towards the ground

wheel and axle simple machine made up of a wheel on an axle, used to turn or lift objects

FIND OUT MORE

Books

How Machines Work: The Interactive Guide to Simple Machines and Mechanisms, Nick Arnold (Running Press, 2011)

How Things Work: Simple Mechanisms, Ade Deane-Pratt (Wayland, 2011)

Put Levers to the Test, Sally M. Walker & Roseann Feldmann (Lerner Classroom, 2011)

Websites

www.edheads.org/activities/simple-machines/index.shtml
Discover more about machines on this website.

www.explainthatstuff.com/toolsmachines.html
This site has some useful diagrams to help explain all about simple machines.

www.galaxy.net/~k12/machines
There are plenty of simple machine projects to try on this site.

www.msichicago.org/fileadmin/Activities/Games/simple_machines
This fun cartoon game is based on simple machine puzzles.

INDEX